ELEGY ON
INDEPENDENCE
DAY

1984
Agnes Lynch Starrett
Poetry Prize

Elegy on Independence Day

Arthur Smith

University of Pittsburgh Press

Published by the University of Pittsburgh Press, Pittsburgh, Pa. 15260
Copyright © 1985, Arthur Smith
Feffer and Simons, Inc., London
Manufactured in the United States of America

Library of Congress Cataloging in Publication Data

Smith, Arthur, 1948-
  Elegy on Independence Day.

  (Pitt poetry series)
  I. Title. II. Series.
PS3569.M47E4 1985   811'.54   84-29783
ISBN 0-8229-3513-9
ISBN 0-8229-5371-4 (pbk.)

Acknowledgement is made to the following publications for poems that originally appeared in them: *Chicago Review* ("Quarry, 1962"); *Crazyhorse* ("Cool Wash"); *Domestic Crude* ("Good-Bye. Sweet Dreams. Come Back," "Tea Rose," and "Two Rooms"); *The Georgia Review* ("Lullaby"); *The Missouri Review* ("In Winter Light"); *The Nation* ("Elegy on Independence Day," "In the White Fog," and "Wrecking Detail" under the title "Wrecking Crew"); *The North American Review* ("Summoned: A Baptism"); *Northwest Review* ("Crosscut"); *Rapport* ("Carpenter"); *Road Apple Review* ("Glove"); *The Seattle Review* ("November Elegy"); *Southern Poetry Review* ("Crescent Lake" under the title "Mosquito Lake"); *Stand* ("Coal" and "The Silence in Virginia" under the title "Cutting").

"Twelve Pole" and "Pictures from the Floating World" are reprinted by permission from *New England Review*, Vol. VII, No. 1 (1984), copyright © 1984 by Arthur Smith. The poems "Nap," "Tarantulas," "Those Goats," "Lines on a Tenth Anniversary," and "Extra Innings" appeared originally in *The New Yorker*. "Pike's Head" and "My Father's Garden" first appeared in *Three Rivers Poetry Journal*, copyright © 1984 by Three Rivers Press.

I am especially grateful to the American Academy and Institute of Arts and Letters, Change Inc., and the PEN American Center for their assistance, and to the National Endowment for the Arts for a grant which aided me in the completion of this collection.

The publication of this book is supported by grants from the National Endowment for the Arts in Washington, D.C., a Federal agency and the Pennsylvania Council on the Arts.

For Ronnie, in memory,
and for my mother and father

CONTENTS

I

II

III

I

TARANTULAS

If you fear them, you can find them
Everywhere in the early autumn evening,
A thick leathery button for a body,
The stiff legs bristling, high-stepping
Under the lawnchair left on the porch.

Turned, or tipped over with a stick,
The tarantula homes in, and once again
Starts up, uglier for being undeterred.
He understands as little as you do
What pulls him forward, to what end.

When the lighter fluid snaps, he walks
Awkwardly in a half circle, burning and
Bearing the flame, a rainbow, grounded.
The shell won't go. His only burden
Is to be consumed from the inside out.

Smaller, dark, the female crouches,
Trapdoor like a penny dropped in dirt.
If you lift it and the webbing pays out
To a nest, you'll have them, hundreds,
Bone-white and free, teeming in the heat.

SUMMONED: A BAPTISM

What I remember is a glass-fronted tank
From which, on Sunday evenings, the dead rose
Stubbornly, pinned in their long white robes
That flowed like pleated marble. After the last,
The side windows of the hall were turned out,
And the summer evening air, lifting, loaded
With cut timothy and a pink wash of sky,
Came through easily and almost sweetly,
As though melons had been sliced open outdoors
And the cool meat laid, sugary, on the concrete.

If the spirit failed to take, that first time,
Back into the warm water we went. I went once
Because I lied. She had looked, hard, and cracked
Me on the forehead, hard, the failure of flesh,
Even for love, in her sight ugly. The dull pain
Stayed, though her eyes and the room, my room,
Went small and bright. This woman, with my mother's
Face and hands, glared at the ceiling as though
Beyond, at God, and then while she cried, again
Struck me. The pain, I said, and still say, stayed.

My mother's dream, returning as though summoned,
Wakes her in a pale light. The laying on of hands
Has done no good. She calls me to the bed,
Resigned, no longer expecting to be released,
And tells me someone has been singled out,
Someone, like myself—she can't say who—
Laid out on a kitchen table, covered with a sheet.
She enters, and the room is gray. An oil lamp
Hangs above the body. This, she says, is a sign
Someone is about to join the dead. She can't say who.

4

All of us, good news, were saved, which is
To say we must have suffered, at a critical time,
A low-grade fever, with none more heated
Than the one that brought me down in front
Of an oak dresser, mirrored, into which I could
Not look, the words, like any words frequently
Repeated, a warm, hushed babble in my throat.
If suffering, like any fire, was its own reward,
Then we were all in love, returning to that tank
Repeatedly, burning, and out of breath, burning.

TWELVE POLE

for my mother

You could look a long time for the place, she says,
And I can see her stopping, bewildered,
The engine overheating in the steady rain

And the gravel blue-streaked and milky,
Trickling out into the pines
And an undergrowth of chokecherry and poison oak.

She might never find her uncle
Buried in 1918 in the woods of West Virginia,
What with the weather and the shortness of her stay

And her eldest brother's indifference
With directions. But she can wait. She's counting
On the resurrection of the body and suffering

Redeemed at last, the dead radiant but blurred, rising
From the places few remember—Twelve Pole, Two Gate—
Rising as though robed with fog.

It may be as she says, that belief
Begins in poverty or fear, in the vernacular
Of a child at nightfall

Followed through the woods
By something she knows only the name of—
A haint, an apparition that might be bearing

The incidentals of a death
Or a bunch of bittersweet custard apples
From the pawpaw tree. And it may be the apples

Or the anguish, or their apparent disparity
That makes her stop, breathless and propped
Against a maple, seeing

6

For the first time the path home
Spiked with ribgrass and the night gathering
Upward from the earth.

On up through the limbs still heavily leafed,
She might see a few stars, unconstellated and nameless,
Firing, when she thinks of it, in all directions.

WESTERN ROLL

30, 40, 50 jumps
A day, from the frost
Of February into summer,
And I never got it right,
That little leg lift
At the top, hanging
Motionless over the bar.
I was 12. Everywhere
I looked were walls,
Heights I hadn't cleared,
And I dreamed of sailing
Over six-foot cyclone fences
And the roofs of cars.
Or I stopped, tired anyway,
Waiting out the rain
Under a gutter bagged
With leaves, imagining
It up at 7'4" or so
And off on another chase,
This one a relay
By way of Weldon Avenue,
Carrying on with a torch
Toward Rome or Athens
And the next Olympics,
Toward Brumel who waited
Already there, lonely
And lovely with his records.

I waited, too, for the clouds
To boil over and move on,
And then was up against
A slippery grass field
And a pit of wood shavings
With all the give of cement,
The bar at personal best,
Working a smooth approach
And hearing the plant foot
Slap the packed earth,
And then the body flushed
And soaring with effort,
Heady and beyond itself,
Caught up with being
Up in the air.

EXTRA INNINGS

Back then the ballpark grass was so overgrown
        and sweet-smelling, I think
I could have bellied down near the dugout
And drowsed away the afternoon. He was, then, simply

Someone on the mound. I went one-for-three—
The single, along with a strikeout and a towering pop-up
        that was, as one wit quipped,
A home run in an elevator shaft. Four months later

He was called up by the Mets. The rest, as we say,
        is history. We say a lot
Of stupid things. We know our bodies are not luminous
        like the stars,
And so we make amends: we think ourselves luminous
        the moment

Sleep comes on, or after loving someone loved—
        that warmth
Radiating out like sound, a name called and carried off
        on the air—or,
Better, and far richer, because it happened once,
        after breaking up

A no-hitter by Tom Seaver, with two out in the ninth.
That was almost twenty years ago, and here I am again
        rounding first, braking,
The dust whirled into a flurry at my feet and the relay
        coming back in

To the pitcher, who has turned away, his face now blurred
        beyond recognition.
Whoever he is, Seaver, or someone nameless like myself—
        a landscaper, perhaps,
As good as any other, catching his breath under an ash tree
        on a new-mown lawn—if he remembers anything,

10

He'll remember the sun flowing the length of his arm
    before flaring out
Into a slider no one could touch all afternoon.
He'll remember his no-hitter as precisely

And firmly as I remember spoiling it, and neither of us
    is wrong. Seaver has his stats,
And the rest of us are stuck with rearranging, cutting
And mixing, working day and night, in dreams, in the dark
    of a warehouse

Stacked with the daily, disintegrating rushes of 20 and 30
    and 40 years ago,
Trying to make it right, remixing, trying to accommodate
    what happened with what
Might have happened. And it never turns out true,

The possibilities not to be trusted but, rather,
Believed in against the facts—whatever they are:
    the low liner hanging
Long enough for the left fielder to dive for, tumbling,

And the graceful pop-up
To his feet, the ball visible, clearly,
In the webbing of the glove held

High over his head, the third out, the proof
That this, ah, yes, this is what happened, the fans in
    his memory standing,
Roaring in disbelief, and the lovely applause lasting
    till he's off the field.

QUARRY, 1962

I've been asleep, lulled
By wind and backup bells
Clanging in the dark.
In a small room clouded
With smoke and dust
We've been all night,
My uncle and I, waiting
For the truck to be loaded
With Arizona rock. Over beers,
Over tins of sausage and potatoes,
He's been laughing
About his three wives,
The many jobs, the year
Burrowed on a snowbound hill
Somewhere in Korea.
Now, he is saying, Now
You'll see them,
And he means women,
The real stuff at last
Cooing and waving, coasting
By the rig,
Their dresses hitched.

And so the diesel's thundered up
And the chrome wheels wiped
Free of dust.
I crawl into a cab
Smelling of tar and rubber
And start that long delicious roll
In which I see myself forever
On the road, loaded,
Climbing through the gears,
The distant hills of California
Pink in the early light,
My face against the window,
And the window whitened
To a flat cloud
On which I float high over
My home town, and my home,
And my mother
Smaller and smaller
Calling from the porch.

WRECKING DETAIL

120° on the roof, or what's
Left of it,
My father hovers above me
Cracking loose the charred rafters.
The ashes float down,
Filtered with every breath.
I was going to lay it out
This morning, tell him
I'd had enough of sweeping insulation
And chips of glass
Scattered over the floor,
Of coughing up blackness,
Of being able
Only to eat and drop, as numb
As a button lost for years.

Now it's almost two.
Each room is poured in heat
And I haven't said a word.
I've been waiting for the right moment
To lay down my father's version
Of the future, a future
I can taste already,
Salty and ashen,
Especially while the sun
Burns through the stacked clouds
And the blue planes climb
In a slick maneuver, bunched
And then trailing off
From one another, five sleek jets
Banking for the green hills.

NAP

Waking at dusk, the room
Red with the last
Light of summer, I leave
Her sleeping and walk out
On the screened porch.
North, above the hissing
Power lines, a sky studded
With clouds, hailstones
Ticking the tin awning,
And the smell of a crushed rose
Rising from the grass. I thought
I would never age, but seeing
Her face swollen from lack
Of sleep, I saw my mother
Once again crossing
The corner lot, home
From the cannery at dawn,
A bag of plums and peaches
Cradled in her arms, her face
Lined with the night.
I remember a rush
Of sunlight flooding
The open door, her clothes
Dropped down the white hamper,
And the cool, stiff covers
Turned back. And then
She slept, and I slept,
And the day went
On and on.

MONOPOLY

All night, while cousin Willie and I hunkered down
Crosslegged around the board, rolling and tapping out our moves,
    I was half afraid
One of us would billow up in flames.

Willie knew everything, her first year
Of sixth grade, about the spontaneous combustion
    of human beings,
And was right, I figured,

About the odds being
    two to one. It happened
Or it didn't. Life can be simple when you're twelve
And aware of nothing but the passion
    inherent

In being alive, a lust so acute and self-centered
    you wouldn't mind
Blazing up, momentarily, in its brilliance.
It wouldn't have mattered, then, if Pop came in, drowsy
    in rumpled underwear,

And found only his wide-eyed boy, and knucklebones and ash,
    and the carpet charred
Where she'd been sitting. That night
She was lucky. She bought up almost all there was, and won,
    and wasn't fired-up

As some sort of sacrifice to the intensities
Of youth. Willie believed in those metaphors of glory,
And now she's dead, and it matters

That she was wrong. The odds, I think,
    are one to one.
It happens, though for most of us the stuff of glory's
Hammered out so thin,

And over so long a period of time, that the lead
        it's hammered against,
More and more, shows through, and we call it
Tedium, or sadness, or whatever

Distinguishes the lives most of us clock into and out of
From those others—apocryphal
Or real, like Willie's—

Those abruptly ended lives we nourish and tend to,
As one way of dealing with the earth, and with the loved
        debris
We bring to it.

II

ELEGY ON INDEPENDENCE DAY

Over the balcony eave, seaside,
One after another, the rockets arc
Barely into view, each sudden thud
Rolling from behind the brickface.
We used to say the rockets "burst,"
As though speaking of someone's heart—
Star-beam, dream-light, bright spokes
Wheeling, falling in a sort of glory.

One summer, in an orchard in Manteca,
The scent of peaches was like fog,
The dust rose and settled like fog,
And both of us went waving sparklers.
You ran on, out farther, tracing
Spirals high in the air. They stayed
Long after the light went, after you
And the heavy, sweet trees were one.

Now I close my eyes and find only
Traces of those wiry figures burned
Into the night. They are fading as
They must, and as they always do.
Whatever shines, however briefly,
We tend toward and love perhaps,
Grounded as we are in the literal—
The powder, the ashes, the earth.

GOOD-BYE. SWEET DREAMS.
COME BACK.

A porchlight flared over the lawn,
And you were just in love, leaving,
Your whole body bronze.

You had planned to go on
Counting houses down the block,
Cross over at the frosted lamp,

And then look back.
As she should have been, she was,

Forward on the porch,
Waving good-bye, yours.

All you could think of then
Was growing old beautifully together,
Down the years,

A lane of oaks first- and second-growth,
Sparrows that had been
Chattering and boxing in the leaves

Long since settled into grass and fluff.

In the cold, in her yellow cotton dress,
She couldn't stay, and was gone

By the time you stopped and
Turned to see her, as she should have been,
Dark and forward, back-lit, waving.

LULLABY

So I came into the room
And calmed you back to bed.
It was simple. Your hands opened
On the quilt,
Your breathing eased
In the thin light, and still
I stayed. I was afraid
You would awaken
To a long morning
With the sun in question
And the sky stalled
With its load of clouds,
That your dream of dying
Would at last stun you
With the ordinary,
That you would see the stars
As particular as they get.
If I had known
How to tell you that we live
On those particulars,
On one another,
I would have stayed
Longer at the window
And listened to your breathing
Come and go. I would have
Promised you another day
Smoldering in a pasture of fog,
And a horse stopped
Under the empty trees,
His plumes of white breath
A thinning ladder
Rising higher, and higher,
Through the limbs.

CRESCENT LAKE

Saturday and Spring,
The red hills webbed with vetch,
California poppies burning
All the shades of gold.

Below in the cove, rolling and bobbing,
The smooth lengths of driftwood
Pile against the rocks.
On a hill of Queen Anne's lace, my wife

Walks off into the pale white blossoms,
And suddenly I see her not dying
As we all are,
But already dead.

Across the hill, weeds
Fatten in the noon light.
The wind stops.
She's gone.

LINES ON A TENTH ANNIVERSARY

What she's wearing is the brightest thing in the kitchen,
And that's not much. She's ironing, the iron

Puffing out its own white clouds above a skirt.
I've stopped reading about the broken parts

Of men in the wet assembly lines
And the man with a carnation at his throat

Who wants to sell us the necessities of life.
It is good, I think,

To be sitting in a warm room
While the lawn whitens with frost.

It is good, too,
Still to be in love,

Or whatever
That tune has come to through the years.

THE SILENCE IN VIRGINIA

I found silence in Virginia,
A covered bridge.
Shrubs crowded
Most of the road, and branches
Hummed in the stream.
Fireflies surfaced and were gone.
I sat on the damp bank breathing
The green air, watching the evening
Fan out from the trees.

Above the birches, a nighthawk
Sliced through the dark rounds,
And I was carried
Back to those memories
Of us walking a new way, hand in hand,
Of how I left you in the fog
And drove all night,
And how, outside Oakland,
A Salt Lake station burst
Through static.

In that silence, I wept
Simply and heavily into my hands,
And my shirt rocked in the dark.
You were in the car above me, waiting,
And we were both alive.

NOVEMBER ELEGY

And then the air warmed,
A wasp blundered at the window,
And she felt well enough
To go out for a walk.
If I were tired
Or wanted myself excused,
I could have blamed it
On the shorter days beginning
Brokenly, and slowly
Falling into place.
Now, finding her out
Without me,
A red sweater
Among the grays and browns,
I'm afraid she is walking away forever.
That's how I think
Anymore, worried
And scattered by the simplicities,
By a crystal in the sun
Casting light far
Into the far room where I was napping.
I know only
I've just awakened.
Whatever else that means,
It means the light
Tuned to its few colors, a day briefly
Sweet and warm, the woman I think I love
Gone, in a red sweater.
Every day I see
This clearly—

We are closer to something
Cold and plain, like a window
And the life we see passing
Through that window.
If we see this life at all
We see it breaking down,
Small and here, and there
And gone, we find it all
The more beautiful now
That we see it breaking.

IN WINTER LIGHT

For months I was living only to be worried
With you, and each evening as I waited
Outside your dreams, I thought over
And over again, Nothing will come of this.
This is the good of your life.

Now I am alone, finally, facing your grave
And the background foothills rising, at dusk,
Yellow and deep brown, bruised with pines,
And I don't know how anyone survives.
Nothing has come of it, though someone

Has left a daisy spinning on its wire stem,
As though that could make a kind of sense
Of the life and death that would undo me.
Turning, the petals blur, endlessly white,
The rim of a wheel, the center of which

Also turns, more slowly. In winter light,
The light of grief, against the squares
Of laid lawn, the petals glow. They look
As though they could go on for years,
Or die out with the wind, each wind, or both.

TEA ROSE

If it grows at all, it grows in early March
      Alone, by a field, stubble
          And partly plowed,
The sadness of its salmon-colored buds
      Apparent in perspective.
          From the other side,

Looking back, toward what soon will be remembered
      As her life—the gardens, walks,
          The screened porch
Where one summer the piled-up Santa Rosa plums
      Sweetened the air for days—
          The rose is central.

It's hardly dawn. I've been up and troubled,
      Torn by what she suffered and
          Survived, by what
Dies, and what lives on. Slick and clustered,
      Magenta, the leaves turn,
          And turn again

With the wind, like fish wallowed in a current.
      I hadn't thought that time
          Could show the loss
I feared most, in all its waste, as something
      Less than final, though now
          I find it focused

At the end of winter in a tea rose, so single-minded
      In its mindlessness that all the rest
          Follows in its course.
New growth, I think, and I'm empty and at ease.
      And now the leaves roll pale,
          And that too passes.

COOL WASH

Jesus, it wants to break your heart,
This weeping and dipping into the well.
And so I turn from the tea rose,
Tree heart, all the photos laced
With the dry ice of memory,
And walk out under them, the stars.

Often, they seem a spare comfort,
Almost calm with distance, at least
As soothing as the glow cast up
From the valley, or the cars left
Bluing in the moonlight
Like cakes of ice, gone by noon.

Under roofs or in the cool wash
Of the stars, we are laid out
And bathed, though we rise and fall
And rise again, without intention,
Played over by lights
We thought at one time blessed us.

IN THE WHITE FOG

I've been stupid with her blindness,
The squall of her dreams,
Whatever she thinks of as a tree.

We were always falling, down or out,
Blind in a way. I think
It was an oak. The trick was

Not to shinny back out
On the same slick limb.
If you climbed high enough, straight

Up the trunk,
And crawled into a crow's nest, you were on
A ship. For years

You swayed in that high window
Without a thought, without a sound,
The sun kindling

A hundred small fires
In the waves. You were bound
To discover land.

What you hadn't counted on
Was someone going over
At the last minute

To that other world, the one
Without a referent, in which
Circuses and storms are variations

Only in the weather.
You are sad, too far removed to do anything
But wave.

There is no rescue. Even now
Someone is rocking in the white fog, like a buoy,
Like a buoy, even now.

HURRICANE WARNING

I still have, somewhere,
A photograph of her
    and me leaning out over a balcony railing,
Behind us, I remember, the bay windows
    wickered with tape

And the sky spanned
By a single cloud, its underbelly, here and there, smeared
    with that blood-orange hue
We once saw a field of poppies take on

Just before dusk, in the foothills
South of Sonora. There were always poppies, it seemed,
    washing up and dwindling to a golden point on a hillside
Otherwise green
    with wild oats and weeds,

Or tawny with them, depending. I don't know
    what might have become of us in time—ten years, twenty,
The two of us walking off, as lovers
Are supposed to, hand in hand,

Toward one inevitability
    or another—but time would have had a chance
To deal with us, in its own sweet time.
It would have brought us pain,
    and lulled

It all away; it would have made the hillsides
And the swaths of poppies
    fronting as crops of sunlight
All the more difficult, in the end, to leave;
    and toward the end, it may have left

Us both alone. Along the country backroads,
Wildflowers luxuriate and strive—snowbells, and buttercups,
And the shooting stars that briefly fan
        their faces to the sun.

You can pull over almost
        anywhere you want, and wander,
And lie back in whatever blossoms you can find.
All around you the hills, like sea swells,
        are rolling in

Or rolling out,
        and the clouds you're gazing at
The same, and there seems to be no end of it, no point
        of reference, or anchor,
Except for the faintly bitter scent of the wildflowers
        you chose to walk through, and lie down in.

III

THOSE GOATS

These are the tropics, unheard of
In the blues, though the rank air's
Heavy with refrain.

Forever, too, is a kind of time,
And you could lie that long
On the tar-pebbled sands, tanning

As though once again ten,
Aloof and tilted
On the roof of a garage, down which

You'd imperceptibly slide, never
Quite falling. It's somewhat touching
The way we see ourselves—

Second and third person,
Future, conditional,
Someone else lathered for the sun,

Now and then turning over
On a beach, so bon vivant the stories
Of the past appear

Beyond consideration, though
They're there, like goats
Penned in a yard. In that stillness

Of dust and dung, they butt
Their heads and romp, they smell,
They couple quickly and crowd

Around the picket gate.
Wherever they are, it's almost evening.
They're about to call you home.

COAL

Twist-tied, emptied
Of caramel sweets,
The Brach's bag darkened
With three chunks of coal.
They had been found,
My mother said, somewhere
Outside Wyoming, West Virginia,
And she handed them
Over to me, in this room,
In the foothills of California.
Today I went back
To those jagged rocks, dull
And gritty, peppering in my hands
As I bobbed
And weighed them, lighter
Than expected. Easily
I returned to those coal-riddled
Hills and hollows she first saw
As a child straying
From the house, the porch
And fence knotted with vines,
Copperheads and water moccasins
Like traps set in the beautifully burnt
Leaves of autumn. All
I could remember of the evenings
Was that they were green and heavy,
That my mother shared a table
With the others, the stories
Jumping back and forth,
Of black lung, of miners
Doubled up on the road to work,

Young bucks riding
Off into the night, torches
Smoking, and a black boy still
Beside a buggy. And back
Farther, the two retarded sisters
Found in a bog, their pockets
Filled with stones, and back
Farther and farther they went,
Until there was only
Silence in the room,
And the shuffle
Of those hooded trees
Moving closer to the house.

PIKE'S HEAD

1.

For weeks I dreamed about them, rainbows
And German browns, the entire workshop
Floored with trout the size of runt tuna,
Their gills clouded over red and orange
And their eyes ash-colored, bottomless,
All gutted and laid out on burlap sacks,
Seventy and eighty and losing count.
It must have been a kind of heaven
To have stood in that garage, a child,
Breathless in the stilled air.

2.

You have to hit them backside the head,
Hard, he said, like this. He held it
By the hind legs, kicking, and I remember
The sunlight faltering through the leaves
When he brought the blade blunt-edge down,
And the neck cracked, and over the block
He flopped it so the jawbone jutted out
Just where the blade went in, pinning it,
While with the hind legs he yanked it free.
There's eight to go, he said. And clean up.

3.

I'd had a couple of beers myself before
He hit her in the mouth. What would you
Have done, your uncle with a backhand
To your aunt, and her down like a rock
And back up fast, breaking the top off
A bottle of bourbon, and lashing it out
And sneering, *like this?* I got sick
And followed him out under the swirling heavens.
He shook his head awhile. He dropped softly
To the ground, a hollow sound, a melon.

4.

If it had hung there long enough, or if
Another had before, he might have seen it
Daily—a pike's head hung on a tenpenny
Barked with rust—and paid it less attention
Than the clothesline strung out from it.
I doubt he ever worried what the source
Of love was, or what a pike's head had to say
To each new generation idling after supper
On a porch, speechless, and stunned a little
With being alive, just as he was, once.

TWO ROOMS

The bed shook,
I heard a whistle fall,
And then an engine
Dragging its heavy sound.
I rose, unsteady
In a small room, the curtain
Lit up like a lamp.
My face cooled
On the window
And the light rushed in.
I remembered how the bus
Idled in its stall,
How the doors folded open
And then clamped shut,
How each time counting the thin bills
I came up short.
I stood there,
At a hotel window
Stitched with rain, staring
While a boy coasted over the walk,
The slick papers skipping
A doorstep at a time.

I had forgotten how small
My old room was,
How near the tracks
My father's house was built,
How often late at night
I woke to boxcars
Rocking on the rails,
To a window shattered with frost
And a fire close
Behind the oleanders,
Those spikes of heat blocked
By shadows back and forth.
I had forgotten how many times
Those men got up and
Sat back down,
How cold they must have been,
And later how they must have swayed
As those freight cars slowed
Into the gray terminals
Of Stockton or Sacramento,
The shapes of men
Flickering in the chutes.

CARPENTER

That winter, dark came early.
I remember halfway home
The leaves that murmured

In a red glow in the gutter,
The cold

Whirring of the tablesaw
In the garage, my father
Leaning over sheets of plywood,
Working.

While the light slanted
Like a ramp of yellow glass
Up to the roof,

I was on my knees
Piling the shavings,
Gathering nails

And marbles of pine sap.
When he was done, high
On his shoulder
I went flying,

My ear brushing
The fluorescent lamp

That hummed against the rafters.
Into the warm house,
Into the bright kitchen we went

Where the smell of doughnuts
Hung from the ceiling.

CROSSCUT

And after that short high ride
On his shoulders to the house
He set you down, the back steps.
Nothing was left of the day

But a sky roofed with clouds
And the smell of the cold wood
He had all night, and most of the day,
Worked with. If you learned,

Were learning what to know
Of maple, oak, and sugar pine,
Of fourpenny and drop-forged,
The difference in ball-peen and claw,

It was not a secret you learned
Slowly. This was work. This
Was repetition to be turned
Daily, like a stone, to a man's

Advantage. Of this day, nothing
Was left but the sound of the wind
And dry leaves stacked in the gutter.
You stood at the window, hands numb.

At first, it looked as though your father
Were raking darkness into piles.
Everything you touched was cold.
Everything was waiting to be touched.

GLOVE

Earlier, as the evening
Spread over the stubble field
And the moon beamed
Above the pines, half
Silly, half in love with
The freckled cows trudging
By the yard, I was thinking
Of the child I used to be,
Sleeping the way I used
To sleep, in the glove
Of darkness. Once,
Before that drowsy lull
And deliverance, I
Stood in a dirt alley
Bordered by weeds, watching
The evening descend in layers,
Each one heavier and darker
Than the last, peeling
And falling until the moon
Rose, burning at the core,
And the trees went white,
And the insects
Began in the grass.
When I looked
Back at the red road
It was gone, the rain
Staggering from the woods,
A porchlight pouring copper
On the fallen leaves.

Bareheaded, cold
In an early shower,
I returned to a house
That once stood for joy,
For something I'd almost
Known, only to find a door
That wouldn't budge,
The lights on,
And no one home.

MY FATHER'S GARDEN

Nothing in the cinderblock planter
But beefsteak tomatoes, half a dozen,
Green, the kind going four for a dollar
Off the dewy flats outside any Safeway.

His first garden at 65, he's had enough.
Pointing past the hurricane chainlink
He shakes his head—burdock and burr clover,
And foxtails, legion, tanning toward seed.

Every damn morning, he mutters, rabbits,
And birds from the field, and tumbleweeds
Like children nosing where they shouldn't,
Their fingers hooked through the fence.

Like me, he's afraid of the wrong things.
Still, when he sweeps his hand out over
The field, the plants and animals, if only
For a moment, all bow down and are hushed.

PICTURES FROM THE FLOATING WORLD

They were never meant to last,
Woodcut or print, the press steadily
Blurring detail, the point lost

In process. I remember reading
Of hundreds from a single run
Stacked like tissue paper

In assembly lines, wrap
And filler for crates of porcelain
And wooden trinkets, thickly lacquered,

Exotic only as they neared
The shores of other floating worlds,
England and elsewhere. In Hiroshige's

"Evening Snow at Kambara," the sky
Is so laden, so much a natural occurrence,
The peasant who happens to be walking by

Brings, by default, the snowscape
Into focus. I can only wonder
What weighs him down—age or fatigue, or just as likely

The loss of a wife or child he might never
Speak freely of. His woven hat,
Like his reticence,

Stands out like a hay rick in a mown field,
And except for the tracks
His wooden clogs have left in the snow,

There is little difference
Between what stretches ahead of him
And what he has walked on past,

One step and another, his head lowered,
Almost bowed, to the heavily layered hillside,
And his body doubled over,

As though the snow suspended in those clouds
Had already settled on his shoulders,
Or was about to.